SHAW - GRIFFIN TAVERN, Est. 1804

An Early National Road Inn

Marci Lynn McGuinness

Shaw - Griffin Tavern, Est. 1804, An Early National Road Inn
Marci Lynn McGuinness

ISBN: 978-0-938833-64-2

This book and its historical research were sponsored by Phil Holt, owner of GNH Trucking, 4684 National Pike, Farmington, PA, and the historical Shaw-Griffin Tavern.

www.gnhtrucking.com

Marci Lynn McGuinness
Author/Screenwriter/Historian/Ghostwriter

Shore Publications . 304 698-6207
P. O. Box 242, Chalk Hill, PA 15421
shorepublications@yahoo.com

Purchase the book:
www.amazon.com/author/marcimcguinness

The Shaw - Griffin Tavern Cover Photo (and two others) were contributed by Darlene Holt Lint.

The year of the cover photograph is unknown, but notice the front porch signs, "Beer" and "Bath".

TABLE OF CONTENTS

Preface

The Holt family has owned the Shaw-Griffin Tavern at 4630 National Pike, Farmington, Pennsylvania longer than either Shaw or Griffin. In Phil Holt's lifetime he remembers a salon being run in the building and a few people living there off and on, but as the years zoomed by like the traffic, this historic relic became uninhabitable.

The National Pike that was once its bread and butter was encroaching and eroding the old stone inn every minute of every day. So in 2022, owner Phil Holt hired the Wolfe House & Building Movers to preserve the inn by moving it 150 feet away from the National Pike.

At this writing, the 522 ton stone chunk of history is 218 years old. The Holt family has owned it since 1914, 108 years. The Griffins ran it as a wagon stand, inn and tavern for 61 years. The Shaws owned the land 19 years before opening the inn. They lost the place to the state and Andrew Stewart bought it in 1816.

I have dug through journals, deeds, maps, census, birth, genealogy, death, marriage and military records making discoveries and putting together the story of the inn per the information available. I wish I had a few stories from people who knew the Shaws and Griffins, but those days and folks are long gone.

Marci Lynn McGuinness
Author/Historian/Screenwriter/Ghostwriter

Nemacolin's Path, Braddock Road, the National Road/Pike

When Chief Nemacolin ventured through the mountains of southwestern Pennsylvania, he could not have imagined that the path he worked so hard to create through the dense forest would one day be a much traveled tourism route.

General Braddock and George Washington used the path in the mid 1750's. Troops widened it, and once Braddock came through, it was renamed Braddock Road. Braddock was buried in this road just west of his Twelve Springs Camp which is part of the Shaw-Griffin Tavern original land tract.

In 1812, Thomas Faucet was 92. He hiked through the woods from Kentuck Mountain (above Ohiopyle) and showed Abraham Stewart, Wharton Township Road Supervisor, where General Edward Braddock was buried.

Many parties had hunted for the grave over the years, but it took the man who claimed he shot Braddock to share that information with the public. Faucet was a huge mountain man. The original BigFoot! Old books say that he killed many travelers for their money and horses. He lived to be 109 years old.

Abraham Stewart's son, Andrew, was with his father that day and witnessed this historic event, helping to move the bones. He was 21 years old, working his way through law school. Andrew Stewart almost became President of the United States later, but that is another story.

Before the National Road was built, John Hayden transported a one-ton wagon-load of merchandise from Cumberland to Brownsville. The Braddock Road was a mere path in 1788, riddled with stumps and holes and quite treacherous. It took him a month to make the trip!

Henry Clay and Albert Gallitin fought long and hard for the National Road, but Congress didn't approve the plans until 1806. It took another five years for the work to begin.

Could the men building the dirt road have imagined that there would soon be 400 taverns serving its travelers? The section of the National Road from Cumberland, Maryland to Wheeling, West Virginia was referred to as the Cumberland Road. It took seven years to build, from 1811 - 1818.

The War of 1812 slowed construction as it cost the government $1,300 per mile and workers were scarce. The Army Corp of Engineers inspected the progress. Cumberland Road was considered the Eastern Division and was supervised by David Shriver.

They dug and filled roads from 12 to 18 inches deep and 66 feet wide with a 32 foot stone center roadbed. It was built by the muscle, sweat and blood of thousands of men. They chopped down trees, cleared brush, pounded rock, dug out stumps, boulders, and ditches with shovels. Inch by inch, freedom was born for those who dreamed of mobility and adventure.

Thieves stole stone at night and wagons tore up their progress, but the National Road was built and had an incomparable heydey from 1811 - 1852. Wagoners were called "Pike Boys" and were known to be a hard working, rough and colorful bunch. They drove their team, transporting for farms and merchants.

Soon, every type of wagon, horse and farm animal filled the National Road and stopped for rest and grub at the Shaw Tavern. Many inns posted a sign on the front door with the "House Rules" and those who broke them were removed. Did the Shaws have such a sign?

After 1815, inns competed for contracts with the stage coach lines. They were also inspected and licensed. A stage stand served stage coaches and upscale travelers. A wagon stand served everyday people and commercial wagoners.

Families ran next to their wagons. At night, most wagoners and travelers slept on the tavern floor alongside the fireplace. Community meetings, church, political gatherings, hearings, and shows were held at inns and taverns as they often served as neighborhood gathering centers. The National Road carried people and commerce from near and far.

Conestoga wagons were the Freight Hauling Trucks of their time, from the mid 1700's to the mid 1800's. They were approximately 18 feet long, 11 feet high and four feet wide. Pulled by a team of six draft horses or oxen, they could cover up to 15 miles each day. Although many people think of them heading west, they had been originally built in eastern Pennsylvania along the Conestoga River in Lancaster County.

The Conestoga style wagon was crafted to haul six- ton loads through harsh conditions like muddy mountain trails and streams. The floor beds were curved upward to hold goods securely and caulked to prevent leaks. The frame and wheels were reinforced with wood and iron. The thick canvas cover served as roof and walls. The wagon also hauled water barrels, feed for livestock, and toolboxes. The driver/wagoner or "Pike Boy" normally walked next to the wagon, rather than "drove" the team from the seat up front.

In the mid 1800's the railroads replaced the Conestoga wagon as the east's primary freight hauler. Conestoga wagons were a big part of the National Road's history, but were too heavy and bulky to travel the cross country trip out west. Those who made that trip did so mostly in covered farm wagons

Stagecoaches were treasured as the fastest mode of transport, traveling up to 70 miles on a good day. Hundreds of people, coaches and wagons passed by the Shaw Tavern each day, many stopping in.

Inns were known for the meals they served and the services they provided. Some were wagon stands for the working class. Others welcomed the upper class stages with fresh beds, although they shared them with up to four people. Mealtime was served family style for 25 cents a plate to the upper classes.

Famous characters, campaigning politicians, preachers and performers were commonplace along the way. Innkeepers and locals were always on the lookout for the rich and famous approaching in their fancy coaches. And the inns were a welcome sight to travelers after a long day on the rough road.

National Pike - Toll Road

From 1835 through 1905 the Federal Government turned the National Road over to the states it passed through. Pennsylvania erected six toll houses to raise funds to maintain the road. There was a second story window in each toll house so that the live – in toll keeper could see who was traveling down the pike. At this time, the name of the road became the National Pike.

The two mountain toll houses were erected in Addison and Farmington. The Addison toll house has been restored, but the one near Braddock's Grave was removed in 1894. The Addison and Searights toll houses are the only survivors of the original six in Pennsylvania.

Petersburg Toll House, Addison, PA.

Notice the Farmington Tollhouse on the left side of the National Pike, center. The right side shows the entrance into the Braddock Grave site. The toll house was built in 1835 and removed circa 1894. I see an automobile heading east, so this must be a postcard from the late 1800's.

On the back of the postcard, it says:
"Hello Edith, All well. Your pad shipped today. Also box candy. Will write tonight. Lots of love, Dad and family."

It is addressed to: Mrs. Edith M. Smith, South Mountain, Franklin County, PA. Feb. 29, 1933

Postcard Contributor: The late Debbie Smith Konechny who grew up by Braddock's Inn, sneaked cigarettes, and smoked them on the Braddock's Grave steps with neighbors.

National Pike Tolls

The wider the wheels on your wagon, the lower the fee to pass through the National Pike toll gates, because the wider wheels caused less damage to the road than narrow ones.

Fees were also charged for animals and pedestrians, but if you were heading to church or in the military, you could pass through free of charge.

When the toll taxes took hold, many drovers found alternate routes to avoid paying "per head" for their stock.

Fees:
Sheep & Hogs – 10 cents
Cattle – 12 cents
Horse & Rider – 4 cents
Led/Drove Horse or Ass – 3 cents
Stage Coach with 2 Horses & 4 Wheels – 12 cents
Extra Horse – 3 cents
Wagons & Wheels :
8" & Up - FREE
6" to 8" - 2 cents
Under 3" – 4 cents

Fine for Non payers - $3. 00

The Shaw Tavern Years

1804 - 1816

On June 24, 1755, General Edward Braddock and his troops set up and named Twelve Springs Camp. It was his 8th camp on this journey. There are twelve springs on the property and the soldiers were most assuredly happy to discover them. Braddock and his men had traveled six miles that day from Squaws Fort Camp near today's Youghiogheny Lake.

It is believed that George Washington and his regiment also camped at Twelve Springs on July 4, 1754 after the deadly battle at nearby Fort Necessity. The Twelve Springs Camp tract sits just west of the Shaw-Griffin Tavern and was part of the original property owned by William Shaw.

After the French and Indian War, southwestern Pennsylvania became so dangerous for travelers that in 1768 the state of Pennsylvania ordered all "unauthorized" folks to vacate the region. The penalty was death!

During the Revolutionary War, the Pennsylvania land office went defunct. It took them some time to get up and running afterward. When they reorganized and opened, they sold 300 acre plots at 5 pounds per acre, offering payment plans. They also paid some Revolutionary War soldiers in land grants and settlers began arriving in the mountains, building cabins, and barns.

By 1800 there were just over 20,000 residents in Fayette County, Pennsylvania. But soon, 200,000 annual travelers used the National Road as it gained popularity.

Shaw Bounty Warrant Property

There were several William Shaws who fought for Pennsylvania in the Revolutionary War, but none of them received warrant lands in exchange for their service. This is why I believe that the following William Shaw built the Shaw Tavern.

William Shaw of Virginia fought in the Revolutionary War with Captain Harry Heth's Independent Company. He was in the Army from 1775 - 1783. In 1780, Captain Heth signed a voucher, turning property over to Shaw because he could not pay him for his service. This was called a "Bounty Warrant". Shaw finally received the Bounty Warrant in 1785, two years after his Army service.

The land where the Shaw Tavern and Twelve Springs Camp are located is shown on the original tract map for Henry Clay Township as a “Warrantee" property. There is no # on the warrantee note on the map like the warranted tracts granted to Revolutionary War soldiers who fought for Pennsylvania. This may be due to the fact that it was a Virginia Bounty Warrant.

These early Bounty Warrant records were conveniently lost in Virginia War Department fires in 1800 and 1814, after the Revolutionary and 1812 wars, so there is little paper trail for this property's early days.

Bounty warrants were also used to entice soldiers to join campaigns. The Virginia Land Office Warrant Act was not passed and enforced until 1788. Those warranted beforehand, like William Shaw, were easily sold on the open market or signed over to heirs.

At the Virginia Library there is a "Guide to Register of Exchange Military Warrants from the Virginia Land Office from 1782 - 1831" on microfilm, but they only have the warrant #'s 1 - 34, 530, and 6795 - 6799 that were found lying around the Virginia Land Office after the 1814 fire. These are most likely warrants issued to soldiers from the War of 1812.

Revolutionary War Soldiers were paid in Bounty Warrant property according to rank:

Soldier - 100 Acres
Ensign - 150 Acres
Lieutenant - 200 Acres
Captain - 300 Acres
Major - 400 Acres
Lt. Colonel - 450 Acres
Colonel - 500 Acres
Brigadier General - 850 Acres
Major General - 1100 Acres

Historical Perspective:

1755 - The year after the Fort Necessity fiasco, General Braddock and his soldiers camped on and named the Twelve Springs Camp property. It was the western part of the original Shaw land.
1768 - Traveling the Braddock Road had become so dangerous due to marauders that the state of Pennsylvania ordered all unauthorized people to vacate the area under penalty of death!
1776 - Independence is declared in the United States..
1776 - 1781 - Revolutionary War
1783 - Fayette County was formed from Westmoreland.
1784 - George Washington proposes a National Road.
1785 - William Shaw receives Bounty Warrant
1794 - Whiskey Rebellion.
1799 - William Shaw paid $78 in property tax for 434 acres here.

The Shaw Tavern was way ahead of its time!

1804 - Shaw Tavern was opened as a tavern, inn, and wagon stand on the Braddock Road.
1811 - 1818 - National Road construction.
1816 - Andrew Stewart purchased the Shaw Tavern and Twelve Springs Camp property and land across the road..
1822 - Stewart's New Fayette Springs Hotel opened. (The Stone House Inn)

1822 - Stewart was re-elected for Congress by giving away watermelons to voters.

1824 - John Griffin bought the Shaw Tavern from Andrew Stewart.

1824 - Henry Clay Township was formed from the east end of Wharton Township.

1826 - Thomas Brown Tavern is built at Jockey Hollow.

1827 - Mount Washington Tavern - Nathaniel Ewing constructed it at Fort Necessity. This property was once owned by George Washington.

1828 - Ben Miller built a two story brick tavern at Twelve Springs Camp adjacent to Shaw Tavern. It was later called the "Marlowe Stand".

1835 - The stone Old Petersburg Tollhouse opens in Addison.

1835 - The stone Farmington Toll House is opened.

1837 - The Rush House - Nathaniel Ewing built it at the crossroads in Farmington. Sebastian Rush purchased it from Ewing.

1848 - Andrew Stewart is nominated for Vice President of the United States.

1848 - President Taylor offers Stewart Secretary of the Treasury position. He turns it down and buys up Falls City/Ohiopyle.

1855 - Stewart Township is named after Congressman Andrew Stewart.

1871 - Stewart succeeds in bringing the B & O Railroad through Falls City/Ohiopyle, starting its first tourism era.

1872 - Stewart passed away at 82 years of age.
1885 - The Griffin family loses the Griffin Tavern.
1894 - The stone tollhouse in Farmington is torn down.

Shaw Makes History

In 1804, William Shaw erected the Shaw Tavern on Braddock Road. The German Colonial style stone inn at today's 4630 National Pike in Henry Clay Township included a stable and wagon yard and was at that time part of Wharton Township.

There were no stone taverns nearby, only forest, trails and log cabins. So, how did Shaw know how to go about retrieving stone and laying it?

The Shaw Tavern stone was held together by mortar made from a combination of red clay, horse hair and lime. Imagine how many men it took to clear the land, ready it, and dig, pound and lay 522 tons of stone, to erect a tavern that still stands proudly 218 years later. It must have taken them years to complete this project.

At that time the southwestern Pennsylvania mountains were unforgiving and inhabited by roughians. But Shaw somehow found skilled labor to build his impressive stone building on a mountain where log cabins were the norm. The workers laid the mortar between the stones, but it was also used to cover and overlap the stones that were not exactly flat or cooperative. Using this process and expertise succeeded in forming strong walls.

If William Shaw spent approximately 16 years on this property, why did he go at the onset of the heyday? Did it have something to do with the War of 1812? These are questions that I can not answer.

He is listed in the 1800 census and the 1799 tax record where he paid $78 for 434 acres, so he must have built a temporary shelter there as they cleared the land and harvested the stone.

Early Stone Splitting Techniques

In the mid to late 1700's, the blasting method was popular for splitting stone and may have been used to extract stone on the Shaw property. But another technique was used from 1790 - 1810, The Plug & Feather.

This often-times produced flat stone more suitable for building. Men drilled up to three, one-inch round holes in a boulder. These were two to four inches deep. Two half-round shims were placed in each hole with a metal wedge between them. They hit each wedge with a three pound hammer until they heard the stone crack. Then they stepped back and let the boulder finish splitting

Flat wedge holes were as common as drilled holes until 1870. This stone-splitting method utilized a cape chisel cutting tool which chipped the hole out rather than drilling it. Holes were placed every four inches across the line of the intended split. They tapped each wedge until a crack was heard. The quarriers then allowed the stone to finish splitting on its own accord.

Shaw Background

The Shaws came from Virginia and built a 522 ton, 2 floor stone establishment out of the wilderness along a muddy, rutted Braddock Road. They also owned Braddock's Twelve Springs Camp which was located at the west end of the property. This soldier must have caused quite a stir erecting such a grand inn among log shanties and rough wagon stands.

There are reports that Shaw started the tavern in 1790, but those dates must be when he began working the land, tavern in mind. Virginia and Pennsylvania still both claimed ownership of the region, but Shaw built and ran a popular tavern and wagon stand from 1804.

They did a good business and were regarded as a reputable house with good meals and a warm fire. Families could sleep on the floor for 15 cents. According to recent research, William Samuel Shaw was born in Virginia in 1755 and died there in 1844. He married Rissie Lou Linn Theopealus (1756 - 1844) in 1777. They buried seven babies and had one child, William H. Shaw (1785 - 1877). He married Thypenia Sarah Baine in 1811.

There is a William H. Shaw listed in the records who was born in 1800 and was buried in Grace Church Cemetery in Fayette County in 1860. He may be the son of William

Shaw who built the Shaw Tavern in 1804, but those records have not been found.

William H. Shaw ran the “Braddock's Run House” in Farmington near Braddock's Grave circa 1830. It was a two-story stone inn built by Charles McKinney. The property was owned by the Dixons in 1894. He also ran the popular Snyder Tavern in the dip west of Chalk Hill for a short time.

The Shaws witnessed the Braddock Road being rebuilt into the National Road (1811 - 1818). They did years of big business and must have serviced the first stage coaches that came through in 1815. Oh, the stories they could tell!

The Andrew Stewart Years
1816 - 1824

Congressman Andrew Stewart, 1825
Portrait discovered by the author in the Stone House attic, 1996.

Andrew Stewart was born in 1791, spending much of his childhood on a farm in Gibbon Glade. He was an ace student and worked hard, saving his money for law school. In 1812, he was part of the National Road crew in Wharton Township when Thomas Faucet showed them where to find General Braddock's remains. Andrew's father was Township Road Superintendent.

In 1815, at 24 years old, Andrew passed the bar and became a Pennsylvania State Legislator.

Stewart Campaigns for Congress at the Shaw Tavern

On May 8, 1816, just four years after he helped move Braddock's bones, Andrew Stewart bought the General's Twelve Springs Camp and the adjacent Shaw Tavern. This included 414 acres, one perch and one road.

Stewart watched the original stone markers being placed every fifth mile in 1816 from the Shaw Tavern.

I have been writing about Andrew Stewart since 1991. He seems to crop up in most of my local history research and here he is again. He has never before been linked to the Shaw Tavern in histories I have read. It pays to comb through the old deeds and original tract maps! They hold nuggets of information when and where you least expect it.

The Shaw Tavern was a popular gathering place, so the ambitious Stewart purchased it and the old Bounty Warrant property from the state of Pennsylvania when it became available.

I could not find many of Stewart's early deeds. He was a lawyer and politician after all, but I luckily discovered information on his Shaw/Griffin property dealings in a court proceeding from 1857 concerning monies owed to him on the Twelve Springs tract.

I could not find the record of how much Stewart paid for the property or who managed the tavern for him from 1816 to 1824. Note that back then, land was signed over in poker games or sold for cash. Several of the Andrew Stewart deeds I found showed that he purchased the lands many years, even decades before recording them in the court house. Cash and gold were king and so was Andrew Stewart. The original tract maps have been very helpful in tracking his early purchases.

The Shaw Tavern belonged to Stewart in 1818 when President Monroe appointed him United States Attorney. He retired from this position when he won his first seat in Congress in 1820. He was a 29 year old bachelor. Imagine the campaign parties that must have gone on within the Shaw Tavern walls.

Stewart served as Congressman for 18 years over the next 26 alongside John Quincy Adams, Andrew Jackson, Abe Lincoln and more. As he joined Congress, he built the Fayette Springs Hotel nearby. Did Stewart's crew learn how to build a stone inn from the Shaw Tavern walls?

This is a 1909 photo of the Fayette Springs Hotel built by Andrew Srewart in 1822. The Fayette Bar Association, to which Stewart belonged, poses on the porch. Stewart, who died in 1872, can be seen in the top hat and tails he was buried in, in the second upstairs window from the left. Stewart's funeral was held at the Fayette Springs Hotel. Over a thousand attended! Many folks have seen the Congressman as his spirit still roams the halls there today!

Originally, the property where today's Stone House sits was a 397 acre tract on both sides of the road, warranted to William McClean on January 9, 1787 and called "Braddock's Bridge". William McClean sold it to John McClean on October 15, 1787. This is the second property young Stewart purchased that had history with General Braddock.

Stewart's Later Years

Stewart remained a single man until he was 44 years old. In 1835 he married Elizabeth Shriver, daughter of the Eastern Division National Road Supervisor, David Shriver. The Stewarts had nine children. They owned over 30,000 acres in Fayette County at the time of his death, including most of Falls City (Ohiopyle) and a block in downtown Uniontown called "Stewart's Row" (corner of Morgantown and West Streets). During his adult life, they owned over 80,000 acres of Fayette County, Pennsylvania.

In 1835, he built his home next to the court house, the Clinton House. Here President Taylor visited him in 1848, offering him the position of Secretary of the Treasury. Stewart turned it down in order to build Falls City.

In the 1840 census, it states that the Stewarts had "10 free white and colored slaves" at their Uniontown home. Andrew Stewart fought to bring the Baltimore & Ohio Railroad over rough ridges through Ohiopyle to Cumberland. He succeeded in doing so one year before he passed away.

Passenger trains stopped at the door of his new Ohiopyle House Hotel, starting the first tourist boom in today's popular outdoor recreation destination. Trains filled the

Youghiogheny River area with city folk, who came to enjoy the Ohiopyle Falls.

In 1870, two years before his death, Stewart bought the Watering Trough property halfway down Summit Mountain from William Downer. It consisted of the watering trough, a cabin, four acres and 37 perches. Downer had received the bounty warrant land in 1824. He was the original owner.

Stewart accomplished amazing career feats and loved the mountains. It is comforting to know that his magic touch graced the Shaw Tavern for eight years as he launched his political, law, and land baron career.

The Griffin Tavern Years 1824 - 1885

John Griffin (1778 - 1826) married Sarah Knotts (1784 - 1859) on June 9, 1810. They came from Kent, Delaware in 1823 and lived at the Twelve Springs Camp tract on the west end of the Shaw Tavern property, renting from Congressman Andrew Stewart and running a wagon stand.

In 1824, they bought the Shaw Tavern, 27 acres and 1 perch from Stewart. There is no recorded deed as reported by others, but I came across this information in a court proceeding document concerning the neighboring property.

This was two years after Stewart opened his new playground, the upscale Fayette Springs Hotel (Stone House) a few miles west. John Griffin changed the name of the Shaw Tavern to the Griffin Tavern and ran it as a stage stand.

John and Sarah Griffin had eight children:
Lydia Ann (1810 - 1837)
William (1812 - 1862)

James Laurence (1813)
Nancy (1816 - 1834)
Mary (1818 - 1841)
Elizabeth (1820 - 1891)
Samuel J. (1822 - 1856)
Rebecca (1825 - 1895)

John Griffin was the son of Samuel (1748 - 1790) and Elizabeth Griffin of Kent, Delaware. Sarah was the daughter of William (1754 - 1830) and Nancy Ann Cessions Knotts (1756 - 1835).

After John's death in 1827, the Griffin Tavern was run as a wagon stand and kept by his widow, Sarah, and son, William.

In the 1830 Fayette County, Pennsylvania census, Sarah Griffin is listed with her father and brother, both named William. They resided at the Griffin Tavern Inn on the National Pike, Henry Clay Township, PA.

In the 1850 Census for Fayette County, William Griffin is listed as Innkeeper at the Griffin Tavern. He was 38 years old. His wife was Emeline (34).

Their children were:
Nancy (13)
Sarah A. (11)
Joseph Price William (9)
Mary E. (7)

Lydia A. (5)
William H. (2)

Later, WIlliam H. ran the tavern with his wife, Sara Margaret "Maggie" Kemp Griffin and her brother, Charles Kemp. Charles Kemp (1838 - 1920) was listed in the 1840 Fayette County census. He died in Wilmington Township, Mercer. PA.

Also listed as residents in 1850 with the Griffin surname:
Sarah (66)
Samuel (28) - Listed as a carpenter.
Rebecca (25)
Rebecca (18) She was a Virginia resident.

In 1830 the Griffins witnessed the 5-mile stone tablets along the National Road being replaced by cast iron markers at every mile of the 90-mile stretch through Pennsylvania. They were made by a Connellsville, Pennsylvania foundry owned by Major James Francis.

In 1837 the new Pike Mail Delivery came through from Washington, D. C. to Indianapolis, IN. The route took 65 hours to complete. When the driver approached a stop like the Griffins, he sounded a bugle to announce that the mail had arrived.

In 1853 the Baltimore & Ohio Railroad reached Wheeling, WV and the Pennsylvania Railroad made it to Pittsburgh. This progress forced haulers from the National

Pike to the rails. Passengers found the trains to be more comfortable, less expensive transportation, but the Griffin Tavern kept its doors open for several more decades.

William Griffin Passes On

On May 25, 1862, William Griffin passed away at the Griffin Tavern and was buried in the Griffin Stand Cemetery behind the inn.

His sister, Elizabeth Griffin Stone (1820 - 1891) took over the inn through 1885. She was married to Jacob Stone (b. 1813). William A. Stone, Jacob's brother, helped manage the tavern.

Jacob and Elizabeth Stone had the following people residing at their inn in 1870 according to the Fayette County, Pennsylvania census. In the census, Jacob Stone is listed as a Farmer and Elizabeth Griffin Stone is listed as "Keeps home".

Children of Jacob Stone and Elizabeth Griffin Stone:

Mary R. Stone was born in 1853. In 1870, she was a 17 year old school teacher.
Margaret E. Stone was 15 and born in 1855.
John A. Stone was 13 and born in 1857. The 1870 census states that he "Works on farm".
James Lawrence Stone was 6 in 1870. (1864-1930)

James Lawrence (32) married Mattie Wentworth (20) at the Justice of the Peace in Confluence, PA on April 4, 1895.

Also residing at the Griffin Tavern and Inn in 1870:

Emma Woodmena was 4 and listed as a daughter of Jacob. She was born in 1866.
Isaac Seese was 22, born in 1848, and listed as "Works on farm".
Masouri Seese, 20, was married to Isaac Seese. She may have been a Turner (1849-1912).

Elizabeth & Gabriel Seese (Resting in Griffin Stand Cemetery) were Isaac Seese's parents. They died in 1874 and 1875 but are not listed as living at the Griffin Tavern in the Fayette County census. Their information is attached to the family records of Elizabeth Griffin Stone, who was still running the establishment in 1882.

The Griffin family worked the tavern over several eras. They had it for just over a decade before the toll houses were built. We know they knew Congressman Andrew Stewart as he sold John and Sarah the property and owned adjacent tracts.

The Griffins experienced the heyday with stage coaches of fancy folk stopping in and Conestoga wagons of produce coming and going. They experienced thousands of head of livestock weekly and saw the railroad take over many businesses. They almost made it to the automobile era.

115
TO
Cumberland
to
Washington
16

Twelve Springs Camp - Stewart, Miller & Marlowe

In 1828 Congressman Andrew Stewart "sold" the Twelve Springs tract to Benjamin Miller. This property sat at the western end of the original bounty land and consisted of approximately 50 acres. Miller was 28 at the time but has been described as an "old wagoner" in history books. He ran a tavern and wagon stand on the property. One wonders if he brewed beer or distilled liquor. His brother, Thomas Miller, was 21.

Benjamin Miller built a two story brick house there. There is no paperwork for the transactions between Stewart, Miller and Marlowe. It seems that Stewart "sold" the land to Miller in a cash payment deal and took it back, "selling" it then to Marlowe.

In the 1830 Fayette County census, Miller was listed as a Farmer. He had 13 "Free white persons" and 1 "Free colored person" living at his Twelve Springs abode.

Miller is buried in the Griffin Stand Cemetery behind the Shaw-Griffin Tavern. He was born on July 13, 1800 and died on May 3, 1882 at 82 years of age. Miller had run for state legislature and lost. I could not discover his exact whereabouts over interim decades, but in 1894 it was reported that he had three grandsons in Uniontown, Ben, Jeff and Sam.

In 1857, David James Marlow passed away. He had lived in the two story brick house that Benjamin Miller had built on the Twelve Springs tract and ran it as a wagon stand. Marlowe was paying Congressman Andrew Stewart $2,300 for this and an adjoining property across the National Road when Marlowe passed away. He had not finished paying it off at his time of death. I could not find a deed but the information I did find was gleaned from other deeds and records. Stewart had to produce a "good warrantee" deed to prove Marlowe's ownership.

William Humbertson purchased said land from Stewart for Marlowe's remaining debt of $1698. This property included 414 acres, one perch and one road. It had been conveyed to Andrew Stewart by the Commonwealth of Pennsylvania in 1816. This deed confirms that Andrew Stewart had sold John Griffin the tract of land where the Shaw - Griffin Tavern sits, but this 414 acres did not include Griffin's tract. It did include acreage on the north side of the road.

Marlowe had run the wagon stand on the south side of the road where he lived in the Twelve Springs brick house.

He also had a watering trough and a stable that could house 100 horses on the north side of the road. Marlowe, who was road superintendent, died in the brick house.

In 1816, Stewart bought 434.75 acres across the National Road from the Twelve Springs and Shaw Tavern property. In 1838, he purchased over 200 acres behind the inn.

1870 - William and Sarah Humbertson sold the 50 acre Twelve Springs tract to Andrew Moyes of Allegheny County for $500.

So, the original tract grew and shrunk for years per Andrew Stewart's unrecorded land dealings. There are some things we will never know.

Shaw-Griffin Tavern & Property Owners, 1885 - 1914

- In 1885, the 296 acre Griffin property was sold by the Sheriff of Fayette County to L. B. Springer and David D. Johnson. I could not find a record of the Griffins owning 296 acres, only the 27 acres and 1 perch bought in 1824 from Andrew Stewart (per an 1857 court document), but they must have purchased more property from Stewart at some point.
- Springer's ½ of the investment went back to the sheriff in 1899.
- On June 22, 1899, David D. Johnson sold the property to Robert B. Hutchison for $4,000.
- On November 4, 1899, Robert B. Hutchison sold the 296 acre tract to Jacob Mainhart of Pittsburgh for $6,000.
- On March 4, 1914, the Sheriff of Fayette County sold the old Griffin property of 296 acres to the

Fifth Avenue Bank of Pittsburgh for $3006. This property had been lost to the Sheriff by the executor of the estate of Jacob Mainhart. Matilda Mainhart was executor of Jacob's estate.

Fifty Acre Twelve Springs Camp tract:

- 1906 - On October 22, Leonard C. and Annie M. Livengood sold the 50 acre western tract, the old Twelve Springs camp, to James D. Portster for $500. The Livengood family was from Cameron, Missouri.
- These folks are also listed on the deed with the Camerons and hailed from Allegheny County: Charles J. and Elizabeth A. Little, Samuel F. and Mary J. Slater, Robert F. and Margaret Moyes, W. E. and Mary E. Moyes, and James Moyes.

The Holt Years, 1913 - 2022

1900 - There were just over 110,000 residents in Fayette County.

1913 - On February 24, the western (Twelve Springs - 50 acres) part of the original warrantee tract was sold to John P. Holt for $1,400 by James D. Portster (widower). Portster was from the borough of Manor in Westmoreland County.

After the Toll Era:
1913 - The National Olde Trails Association was formed to promote and maintain the National Pike.

1914 - On March 4, 1914, the Sheriff of Fayette County conveyed the 296 acre Griffin Tavern property to the Fifth Avenue Bank of Pittsburgh.

1914 - On June 25, the Griffin Tavern property was conveyed to John P. Holt (et all) by the Fifth Avenue Bank of Pittsburgh. In this deed, the right-of-way was 12 feet wide and called "Old Gallagher Road". This deed also included William E. Holt, Charles C. Holt and Robert C. Holt of Ohiopyle.

The Holts purchased 296 acres "more or less" which included the two story stone Griffin tavern/house, barn and other out -buildings.

1919 - John T. Holt (1866 - 1919) died coming home from work at a nearby stone quarry. He was accidentally thrown from a truck and run over.

1920's – The Pike became a part of the Federal Highway System and Route 40. In Fayette County, Route 40 follows a lot of the original Pike route.

1925 - National Road construction was completed from Atlantic City, New Jersey to San Francisco California.

1925 - On June 29, Clara M. Holt (widow), Charles W. and Ethel M. Holt, and Clifton H. and Inez Holt, conveyed 177 acres of the Griffin Tavern property to Victor Holt for $1.

1930's – 1940's – Nearby Flat Rock was a resort area with many cabins and called Elk Park.

1930 - The Fayette County census listed Charles W. Holt as 36 years old, son of Clara Holt. He married Ethel Marie Herring (1896 - 2001) in 1921. Ethel had 10 siblings, became a teacher and lived 105 years. In 1919, she graduated with a teacher's certificate after six weeks of education at the California Teacher's College of Pennsylvania. She and Charles had a son, John P. Holt, who was born in 1923. She retired teaching in 1937.

The Shaw-Griffin Tavern to the left became a home. The Holts farmed the property.

The dirt road immediately in front of the house is the National Road.

12 SPRING CAMP TO BE SCENE OF MARKER SERVICE

Prof. John Kennedy Lacock To Be In Charge Of Ceremony Sunday Afternoon.

Unveiling of the marker at the Camp of the Twelve Springs will take place Sunday afternoon at 3:00 o'clock with Professor John Kennedy Lacock, eminent Harvard historian, in charge of the services. Dedication of this tablet was to have taken place September 5 but ceremonies at Jumonville's grave prevented the unveiling.

The site where the marker has been erected is four miles east of Farmington, located on the farm owned by Mrs. Clara May Holt. The tract of land was originally patented by "Job" Clark, famous tavern keeper during the early years of the settling of this part of the country.

Historians regard the Camp of the Twelve Springs as the most probable location of General Braddock's eighth encampment, June 25, 1755, and also the scene of George Washington's encampment, July 4, 1754, after he marched out of the Battle of Fort Necessity with honors of war. Outlines of the old springs and the tavern are still visible.

The tablet was erected at the expense of Mrs. Holt, who has considerable interest in the historical significance of the farm on which she lives.

Several Fayette county residents are expected to witness the unveiling of the marker Sunday afternoon.

1932 – Mrs. Clara May Holt (1871 - 1940) erected an historical marker on the Griffin Tavern property on September 5. It was set up at the side of the tavern to honor the 200th anniversary year of George Washington's birthday. The tablet told the history of the Twelve Springs Camp and Braddock Road but is missing.

Please note that the Job Clark (1758 - 1842) mentioned in the article never owned the Twelve Springs tract as reported. He opened a log tavern wagon stand across the road from Twelve Springs in 1805 where he had 165 acres, including an orchard. He received the property as a Pennsylvania Revolutionary War Bounty Warrant issued in 1797. This is indicated on the original tract map of Henry Clay Township.

After Clark's death, Andrew Stewart scooped up this property as it was adjacent to his tract. James Marlowe "bought" it from Stewart.

Clark came to the area in 1778 and married Lydia Leonard in 1779. He was the same age as her father, Enoch Leonard. Her mother was Lydia Fish Leonard. They are all buried in the old Leonard cemetery along the river in Henry Clay Township where Enoch Leonard settled in 1770.

Clara Holt was married to John Holt on February 21, 1893. She was the daughter of Rueben and Martha (Cunningham) Leonard of Meadow Run and passed away in 1940 at 69 years old. She was a teacher and encouraged her sons, Charles (1893 - 1976), Clifton (1895 - 1941) and John Victor (1898 - 1981), to locate each of the twelve springs on their property.

Holt's Farm Truck

The Holt's farm truck is a Jeffery/Nash Quad 4 wheel drive. The Thomas Jeffries company built them for the Army from 1913 and 1928. This model was designed to replace the mule and went unchanged for many years.

The Quad was run by a 52 horsepower 4 cylinder engine on a 1.5 to 2 ton chassis. It weighed 5350 pounds. The Jeffries company also produced Rambler cars.

Is that John Holt in the driver's seat? One of his sons? We may never know.

NOTE: A big Thank You to Ira "Skip" Seaton of New Salem, PA for identifying the truck.

* Photo contributed by Darlene Holt Lint.

1950's – There is a quick claim deed listed on this deed to Charles and Ethel Holt dated January 25, 1951. It was granted by J. Victor and Virginia Holt and by Inez H. and Lloyd Chrise.

1973 - Charles W. Holt and Ethel M. Holt sold the property at 4630 National Pike for one dollar to son John P. Holt and his wife, Mildred Holt. According to the deed, it was "177 acres more or less". Charles passed away December 9, 1976.

This deed lists properties that were conveyed to others on the western part of the tract including:

1. Victor Holt - 25 acres and 20 perches were conveyed to Victor Holt on June 29, 1925.
2. Tony Canistra was conveyed 7.80 acres on June 17, 1952.
3. Inez E. Holt Chrise - 94 acres were conveyed to Inez on February 19, 1953.
4. J. Victor Holt - 10 acres were conveyed on May 27, 1966

NOTE: Charles W. and Ethel M. Holt reserved a life interest in the conveyed tract and its right-of-ways.

1976 - The National Road was christened a National Historic Civil Engineering Landmark.

1983 - A new deed was recorded to finalize the estate of Ethel M. Holt. All rights to the property went to John P. and Mildred Holt.

1994 - The National Road in Pennsylvania was dedicated as a State Heritage Park.

2022 -Phil Holt hires Wolfe House & Building Movers of Bernville, PA to move the 218 year old stone Shaw-Griffin Tavern 150 feet back from the encroaching National Pike.

Shaw-Griffin Tavern, 2019

Front view of the Shaw-Griffin Tavern showing Route 40.

East side view of the Shaw - Griffin Tavern, 2019.

West Side of the Shaw - Griffin Tavern, 2019.
Below, Rear of inn.

Shaw - Griffin Tavern, 2022

This photograph collection is from April 22, 2022.

The Shaw - Griffin Tavern is braced up and being prepared to raise four feet off the ground.

Front view as men secure the Shaw - Griffin Tavern to move it 150 feet back from busy Route 40.

Notice the chains wrapped around the Shaw - Griffin Tavern, and the windows blocked for security. Route 40 is only a few feet from the historic inn.

The west side of the Shaw - Griffin Tavern, rising!

As they braced-up the Shaw - Griffin Tavern for moving, land behind it was cleared to make the operation go as smoothly as possible.

Rear of the Shaw - Griffin Tavern. Notice the slab where the foundation will be constructed.

Rear view of the Shaw - Griffin Tavern bracing and the newly laid slab.

Shaw - Griffin Tavern, April 29, 2022

This collection of photos was taken when they raised the Shaw - Griffin Tavern four feet off the ground. It weighs 522 tons. That is a lot of stone!

West and rear view of the Shaw - Griffin Tavern, suspended! Notice the steel corner braces.

Workmen are under the inn, but you can not spot them.

Shaw - Griffin Tavern, June 6, 2022

The Shaw - Griffin Tavern was successfully moved away from Route 40. The inn was built from stone dug from this land and held together with lime, horsehair, and red clay.

Here it sits on a solid block foundation and sports a new metal roof. Front view, June 2022.

West side view.

West side view.

Rear view of the Shaw - Griffith Tavern.

East side view showing the defunct Glisan's Diner across Route 40 (right).

Griffin Stand Cemetery

Just to the right and rear of the Shaw - Griffin Tavern is the Griffin Stand Cemetery. The following photos are the gravestones located there and the captions include information discovered about the earliest cemetery residents.

Sarah J. Griffin, 1784 - 1859

This "S. J. G." tombstone still stands in the Griffin Stand Cemetery. Sarah was the wife of John Griffin. They came from Delaware in 1823 and bought the Shaw Tavern from Andrew Stewart in 1824. Their family owned the Shaw - Griffin Tavern for 60 years.

William Griffin, 1812 - 1862

William was the son of John and Sarah Griffin. He and his mother ran the Griffin Tavern and wagon stand after John passed away.

Gabriel Seese (1816 – 1875)

Gabriel Seese was born in Henry Clay Township to Jonas Seese (1791 - 1855) and Frances Maust (1793 -1828). Gabriel is listed as Secretary of the township in 1864. He married Elizabeth Wheeler Seese in 1838.

Gabriel and Elizabeth had six children: Priscilla 1839 – 1905 Joseph Jonas 1843 – 1867, Isaac 1847 - unknown, Jacob M. 1852 - 1898 (J.M.S. grave), Eloise 1854 – unknown, and Sebastian R. 1859 – 1905.

Joseph Jonas Seese, passed away at 23 years old in 1867.

Benjamin Miller - July 13, 1800 - May 3, 1882

In 1828, Miller built a large two-story brick house on the Twelve Springs property while Andrew Stewart owned it. He was an old wagoner, and kept the stand for a short time.

I have no information as to his whereabouts over the decades, but do wonder why he is buried in the Griffin Stand Cemetery. Did he live on the property somewhere? He is not listed in census books.

B. M. baby grave - Is this Benjamin Miller, Jr.?

You let us beautiful memories
Your love is still our guide
Although we cannot see you
You're always at our side

References

Fayette County, Pennsylvania census books and tax records
Microfilm of *Liberty of Genius* newspaper articles, PA Room, Uniontown Library
Multiple Deeds found at Fayette County Recorder of Deeds
Familysearch.com - All records (birth, death, marriage, military)
Ancestry.com
Newspapers.com
Virginia Land Office
Library of Virginia - State Archives
Pennsylvania Land Office and Archives including original tract maps for PA townships.

The Old Pike, A History of the National Road by Thomas Searight, 1893
History of Fayette County, by Franklin Ellis, 1882
Stories of Fayette County by Walter "Buzz" Storey
A Driving Tour of the National Road in Pennsylvania by Cassandra Vivian
Explorer's Guide to Ohiopyle & the Youghiogheny River by Marci Lynn McGuinness, 2000
Stone House Legends & Lore by Marci Lynn McGuinness, 1996

More Books by Marci Lynn McGuinness

Books published after 2008 available at:
www.amazon.com/author/marcimcguinness

Ohiopyle Cookbook, Eat Like a Local, 2018
Braddock Legends & Lore, 2016
Vivian & the Board Track Boys, 2015 (ebook/)
The Mystery of the Ohiopyle Hotel, 2015 (ebook)
Laurel Highland Legends , 2015
Murder in the Vineyard, 2014
Pam's Cooking with Pam Bendishaw, 2013)
1915 Uniontown "Summit Mountain" Hill Climb Program Reprint, 2013
Murder in St. Michaels, 2013
Ohiopyle, That Little Town, WWII (with Lillian McCahan, 2012)
Speedway Kings of Southwestern Pennsylvania, 100 Years of Racing History, 2011
Yesteryear at the Uniontown Speedway (1996, 2nd Edition 1997, 3rd Edition 2008)
Official Program U.S.A. Speedway, 1916 Reprint (1996, 2nd Edition 2009)
Message of the Sacred Buffalo, 2010
Hauntings Of Pittsburgh & the Laurel Highlands, with Don Wagner, October 2009

Gone to Ohiopyle, Illustrated by Colby Love, September 2009

Murder in Ohiopyle & Other Incidents, Summer 2009

Butch's Smack Your Lips BBQ Cookbook, Spring 2009

Yesteryear in Ohiopyle and Surrounding Communities, Volume III, 2008

How to be a Working Author/Writer (2005; 2nd Edition, Fall 2008)

Chesapeake Bay Blue Crabs, 2004

In it to Win It, 2001

The Explorer's Guide to the Youghiogheny River, Ohiopyle and SW PA Villages, 2000

Along the Baltimore & Ohio Railroad, from Cumberland to Uniontown, 1998

Stone House Legends & Lore, 1998

Yesteryear in Smithfield, 1996

Yesteryear in Masontown, 1994

Yesteryear in Ohiopyle and Surrounding Communities, Volume II, 1994

Yesteryear in Ohiopyle and Surrounding Communities, Volume I, 1993

No Outlet!, 1993

Incidents, 1992

Nanny's Kitchen Cookbook, 1991

Natural Remedies, Recipes & Realities, 1986

The Deerhunter's Guide to Success...from the woods to the skillet, 1985

Natural Remedies, 1984

Unforgettable Poems for Everyday People, 1984
What's Happenin' Around Ohiopyle, 1981)

More Publications by McGuinness
Ohiopyle Life Magazine, 2017 – 2019 (Print),
OhiopyleLife Facebook page 2017 - 2022
Around Ohiopyle Map & News July, 2009-2011
Around Ohiopyle Magazine, 2008
Tying the Knot Magazine, 2007
St. Michaels/Tilghman Coupon Booklet, 2003
Yesteryear Calendar series (1990's)
Yesteryear Press (Newsprint Magazine-5 times a year) 1992 - 2002
Speak Easy Digest (Early 1990's-quarterly)
Naturally Yours Newsletter (1980's)
Movies/Scripts
Yesteryear in Ohiopyle - The Movie, 1990's video
Speed King - McGuinness' screenplay based on Yesteryear at the Uniontown Speedway board track
McGuinness has two agents pitching several of her feature film scripts 2020 - 2022

www.ohiopyle.info

Made in USA - Kendallville, IN
12894_9780938833642
09.16.2022 1252